THE NEW WORLD OF CREWEL

THE NEW WORLD OF
CREWEL

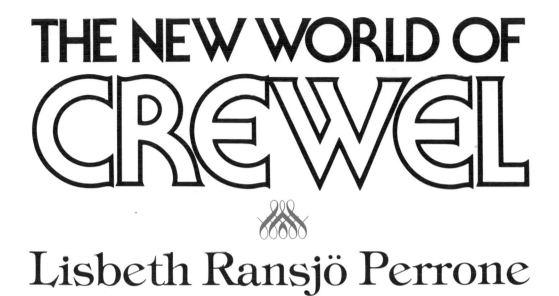

Lisbeth Ransjö Perrone

RANDOM HOUSE   NEW YORK

Library of Congress Cataloging in Publication Data

Perrone, Lisbeth Ransjö
The new world of crewel.

1. Crewelwork. I. Title.
TT778.C7P47   746.4'4   75–10290
ISBN 0–394–48979–9

Manufactured in the United States of America

Color photographs by Neal Slavin
Design by Kenneth Miyamoto

FIRST EDITION

I've heard of wives too musical,

    too talkative or quiet.

Of scolding or of gaming wives

    and those too fond of riot.

But yet, of all the errors known

    to which the ladies fall,

For ever doing fancy work

    I think exceeds them all.

If any lady comes to tea,

    her bag is first surveyed

And if the pattern pleases her,

    a copy then is made.

She stares too at the gentlemen

    and when I ask her why,

'Tis "Oh my love the pattern of

    his waistcoat struck my eye."

—Nineteenth-century poem

Contents

I WOULD LIKE to extend my thanks and deep appreciation to Marianne Steinberg, Ruth Robbins, Barbara Singelton, Muriel Connery, Dorrit Gutterson and Nan Keenan, who have been of invaluable help in working the embroideries; to Arts & Crafts Together, 53 Third Avenue, New York, N.Y. 10003, for blocking, mounting and framing all the embroideries in the book with such skill and craftsmanship; to Eva Costabel for an outstanding effort in translating my designs into fine line drawings for transfers; to all my students, past and present, in whose company I always find inspiration and encouragement; to Susan Brown for the stitch charts; to Thumbelina Needlework Shop, Solvang, California 93463; and finally to my cheerful son Abbott, who is turning into quite an embroidery critic.

Lisbeth Ransjö Perrone

INTRODUCTION

THE EARLIEST-KNOWN relics of embroidery were found in the burial places of Egypt, but samples of ancient needlework can be found in all countries throughout the world. Many historic figures, such as Queen Elizabeth I, Mary Queen of Scots, Charles I and Charles II, Queen Anne, the kings of Scandanavia and, in more recent times, the Duke of Windsor, have enjoyed working with the needle.

I think of embroidery as an enrichment of fabric with the needle, thus samples of fine embroidery can be found in museums and art galleries throughout the world. It is interesting to realize that certain embroideries, though they are very beautiful, are referred to as household or peasant embroidery because they have been made for functional reasons rather than for decoration.

Any work done by hand, with a needle as a tool, can be considered embroidery or art needlework, because the basic stitches—even in making a dress by hand—are the same. The back stitch, the herringbone, buttonholing—these are all functional as well as decorative stitches. The different types and techniques of embroidery are classified depending upon the background materials, the yarns, the designs and the specific stitches used.

In our time, we find people in all walks of life, men as well as women, the old and the young, enjoying the art of embroidery, but for a long time, it was not given the attention it deserved and was regarded as a lowly applied art or an exclusively feminine occupation. However, in Medieval Europe, in the East and in certain countries like Scotland, men have not considered this work beneath their dignity, and it is a pleasure to see that more and more people in our day are opening themselves up to the pleasures of this craft.

Crewel Embroidery

Crewel embroidery is done in crewels—loosely twisted two-ply woolen yarns—worked on a closely woven material such as linen. Crewel, sometimes referred to as Jacobean embroidery, was very popular during the seventeenth century in England during the reign of James I. Most modern crewel pieces are copied from this period, and consequently, crewel is often considered English in origin. However, no style of art is ever solely de-

pendent upon one period of time or one region. The laws of evolution and nature also hold in the arts, and in crewel, the work we do today shows influences of many individual and international expressions.

Early crewel work was usually done monochromatically, and the yarns were almost always locally hand-dyed. The stitches were few and simple, which is not to say that they were less beautiful. In fact, even in modern work the artistic value of very pretentious needlework seems to me to be overrated. I love the Victorian comment I once read: "So much today is done to worry the eye by day and to give bad dreams at night."

In seventeenth-century England, trade with the Orient flourished and provided to the embroidery of the time inspiration from Eastern printed cottons, from porcelain and from lacquered objects. Early English embroideries also reflected the effect of traveling in that parrots, tropical birds and plants like pomegranates and pelicans appeared in the needlework.

One of the best-preserved and well-known pieces of old crewel embroidery is the *Bayeux tapestry*. This famous work tells the story of William the Conqueror and his conquest of England. It measures approximately 231 feet by 20 inches and dates back to circa 1100; 1,572 objects and figures are depicted in 72 scenes. It is believed that the tapestry was embroidered by Norman working people at Bayeux. Whether Matilda, William's wife, had

a part in the actual embroidery isn't really known, but I like to think that she did.

For all its antiquity and great beauty, the Bayeux tapestry is a typical example of crewel embroidery—a work of art embroidered with woolen threads on a linen background. It is a form of embroidery where you are not limited, as in canvas embroidery, to the mesh of the canvas. Every shape you design and embroider in crewel can be treated differently, though it is an integral part of a larger design. For this reason, even though they are worked from the same pattern, no two pieces of crewel embroidery need look the same. Each person doing crewel embroidery can add his or her own touch of shading, of color combinations, and of execution. Some of these variations even come about in trying to cover up a mistake but they only add to the wonderful creative variety possible.

Another advantage of this very creative kind of stitchery is that crewel is a very inexpensive hobby. Even a really elaborate project will cost you relatively little to make. Crewel work is a lively, creative craft which can be done as simply or as elaborately as you like.

Modern Crewel

The patterns in this book have been created out of our own contemporary feeling for design, but of course,

many of the patterns are inspired by the old, unbelievably beautiful traditional embroideries—particularly from seventeenth-century England. To be a part of history, however, we cannot slavishly copy it. We should study the antique and admire it, but adapt what we learn to our own century and to our own environment. In that way, perhaps, we will be creating "heritage" crewel work in our own time and thus making this century one that contributes a great deal to the entire evolution of embroidery.

You, yourself, as you embroider, will be adding to this heritage by creating your own variations and by being open-minded in your work. Don't compare what you do with what already has been done. Instead, enjoy crewel as a personal art.

How to Use This Book

The New World of Crewel is a workbook with about 50 designs for pictures, pillows, chairs, stools, tablecloths, curtains, clothing, bags and eyeglass cases. Each design is shown in a full-color photograph. There is a stitching chart for each pattern and, at the back of the book, a transfer so that you can iron the specific pattern on your fabric.

The designs are intended for beginners, for intermediate embroiderers, as well as for those who are able to do advanced work. Each design is marked accordingly.

At the beginning of the text, you will find instructions on the kinds of tools and materials you will need, as well as instructions on how to choose a design, how to transfer it, how to start, work, and finish a project. Most important, there is a dictionary of the stitches that you will need to do the work in this book, as well as clear instructions for each stitch.

I hope that the material here will help you to explore the almost endless possibilities of combining designs or of using parts of a transfer for a functional or decorative project.

Tools

Embroidery Basket

Keep all your tools in a basket, a bag, or some other portable storage unit. I use a picnic basket for my own work, and some of my students use tote bags or plastic bags.

Needles

The needle is the oldest tool of decorative expression, going back to the early Stone Age. Interestingly, throughout the successive stages of bone, bronze and, later, steel, the needle has remained virtually unchanged in its structure and design.

You should buy crewel needles from your local notion or needlework shop. These needles are thicker than a sewing needle, but finer than a tapestry needle, with a sharp point and an eye that can accommodate the various thicknesses of wool yarn. Crewel nee-

dles generally are sold in a small assorted package which includes needles for one- and two-ply yarns. Make sure that the needle you choose is not too heavy, or it will make holes in your fabric.

In addition to your crewel needle, it is also useful to keep a few blunt tapestry needles in your workbasket for stitches where the thread does not go through the fabric, as in Cloud Filling.

Hoops

It is essential to work on a hoop in most crewel embroidery. Use a hoop with a tight grip, preferably in wood, since metal has a tendency to slip.

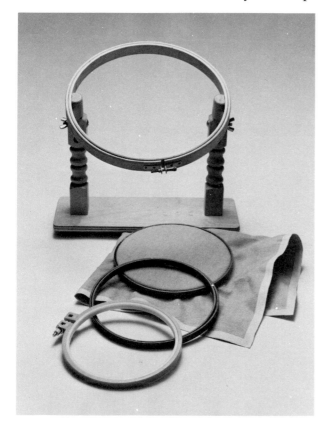

If it doesn't grip tightly it will not give you enough tension, and your work will tend to bunch. Hoops are

available freestanding, in clamp and in hand-held styles. Pick one that suits your budget and feels comfortable for you to work with.

If you have a rug frame that is the size of your fabric, you will find that it is a wonderful way to work. Carefully tape the edges of your fabric and then, through the tape, tack the fabric down to the frame every few inches with heavy push-pins. Proceed

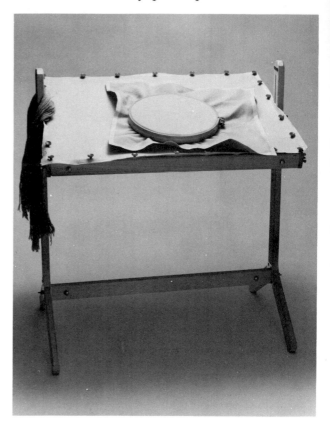

with your stitching. Rug frames are very convenient to work with, particularly when you are embroidering a large piece of fabric.

Thimble

If you are used to working with a thimble, you will need one for your crewel embroidery. Again, there are

no strict rules about such things as thimbles, and you should use one only if you feel comfortable doing so.

Ruler

A ruler is used to help center the design on your fabric.

Pencil

Use a soft lead pencil with a fine point to indicate lines and stitch direction on your fabric.

Tape

I always tape the edges of my material to prevent them from unraveling. Later, when you block your finished piece, the tacks or pins can be placed on the tape, rather than on the fabric.

Push-Pins

Keep a box of rust-proof push-pins or tacks for blocking.

Scissors

A pair of standard sharp scissors is important.

Notebook

Keep a small embroidery notebook for ideas, hints and sources of supply.

Fabric

Crewel embroidery should be done on a closely woven material. Always invest in the best quality fabric. It would be a pity to put a great deal of time and effort, as well as fun, into a sleazy piece of fabric. Stay away from bargains, such as materials that pucker. I enjoy working on traditional linen twills, closely woven square-weave linens or sateens.

Yarns

Crewel embroidery is always done with woolen yarns, although no one is going to be upset if you work any of the designs in this book in a linen or silk thread. Be free—simply call your work linen or silk embroidery instead of crewel.

Choose a yarn that is not too tightly twisted, or it will be difficult to work flat stitches. For all the designs in this book we have used Paternayan crewel yarn, Appleton and one strand out of a three-ply Persian-type yarn. These yarns, or their equivalents, can be obtained from most needlework stores throughout the country.

There is no rule about the thickness of the yarn. One can use one, two or even three strands. The patterns in this book have been worked with one strand, in general, but I would recommend that a beginner start with a small bold design worked in a double strand.

The coarseness of the background material will also determine the thickness of the yarn. In other words, a bold, rough background material will require a thicker yarn, as a fine fabric will require a less coarse yarn.

Bear in mind that when you are doing crewel embroidery on clothing, it is much better to work with a man-made fiber or cotton rather than wool. This will make laundering a lot easier.

How to Choose a Design

First, look around you and decide what object you want to make and the kind of design you prefer. Then, browse through the color photographs to find a pattern you like. Bear in mind that though a design may be shown as a pillow, there is no reason you can't use it differently—as a picture or a handbag, for example. Or you may want to pick up only one element of a larger design to use by itself on a shirt collar or a pillow. If you like, you may choose part of a design and then enlarge or reduce it to fit the item you wish to embroider.

Make sure, particularly if you are a beginner, to consult the work page for your pattern to see whether the design is too difficult for you at this point. Bear in mind that "easy," "intermediate" and "advanced" are only terms suggested as a rough guide, based upon working with my own students. You may find all the patterns easy for you. Once you have selected a design, turn to the appropriate work page for specific instructions.

Starting a Project

Now you are ready to buy the yarn and fabric you will need.

Yarns

If your store sells yarn by weight, $\frac{1}{4}$ ounce of each color is enough for any pattern in this book. If the yarn is sold in skeins, one skein of each color will be enough.

All the shades and colors are noted on the work page for each design. When the work page calls for three blues, for example, you will use different shades of blue. Keep your yarn braided or on a hoop or a coat hanger while you are working so that it does not get knotted up.

Fabric

To decide how much fabric you will need, measure the actual size that the finished piece will be and add $1\frac{1}{2}$ inches all around the edges to allow for blocking and mounting. In other words, for 12'' × 12'' pillows, cut your fabric 15'' × 15''.

Taping

Cover the edges of the material with masking tape after you have cut it.

Transferring the Design

At the back of the book, you will find an iron-on transfer for each design. This transfer can be used on any light-colored fabric. Carefully remove the iron-on pattern you are going to use and spread it out before you. Cut off the identifying number.

Iron out your fabric to make sure it is perfectly smooth. Then lay the fabric neatly out on your ironing board. Turn the transfer, *face down*, onto the place on the cloth you wish to embroider. Most of the time you'll want to center the design on your fabric, but sometimes you may wish to use the embroidery at the border, or, for example, in the corner of a tablecloth or on the pocket of a shirt.

Pin the edges of the transfer securely to the material so that it cannot slip. Now set your iron to the *dry* setting for cotton. Do *not* use a steam setting. If your fabric is a bit heavy, set the iron for linen, but make sure that the iron is not so hot that the paper turns even slightly brown, or else the material will surely scorch.

When the iron is hot, place it firmly on the center of the transfer. Move the iron in half-circular motions until you have covered the entire transfer.

Do not lift the iron while you are transferring or the paper may move slightly and you will get a double line.

Remove the transfer and, if you've worked properly, you will have a perfect duplicate of the design on your cloth.

Tracing

If you choose a dark material, you will have to trace the design onto the fabric instead of ironing it on. This is no particular problem, since tracing is a simple procedure. Buy dressmaker's carbon paper in white or yellow.

Pin the transfer to the fabric as you would if you were going to iron it on. However, pin it only on three sides. Then slip the carbon, *face down*, between the material and the transfer. Do not pin the carbon, or the pins will leave marks on your material.

Trace the designs firmly with a pointed instrument such as a hard pencil. I use a knitting needle held securely in my hand as if it were a pencil. Work on a firm flat surface and make sure to trace every line on the design.

Though it is not absolutely necessary, whenever I am working on a dark fabric, after I've traced the design, I go over the outline of the entire pattern on the material, using white india ink or white acrylic paint. You can buy these in any art supply store and apply the ink or paint with a very fine brush. This sounds complicated and it may not be necessary, but the method will help you in a long-term project where your carbon lines may have a tendency to rub off.

Even when you use the transfers on light-colored fabric, there may be a favorite design you wish to iron over and over again, even after the transfer ink has worn out. In that case, use the transfer method described above, with dark carbon paper on light colored fabric. Pay special attention not to smudge the material. When using this method, take your rings off and try not to rub your hand across the pattern.

The Work Page

Look carefully at the work page for the design you have chosen. You will note that it indicates whether the design is easy, intermediate or advanced. It tells you how many shades of each color the pattern requires, and the stitches used are indicated by a number which corresponds to a number on the drawing. Note that not every line on the chart is marked with

a number. For example, if a branch is unmarked, simply look at the stitch number for the same branch or a similar one elsewhere in the drawing.

Directions for the stitchery and hints on how to work and use the pattern also appear on the work page.

Embroidering

Before you begin, consult the color photograph page to see where each color yarn appears. Tape a piece of yarn right on your transfer to mark the changes in color, or attach the proper color yarn in the right place on the fabric itself.

Next, note on the work page what stitches are used in the pattern. If you are not familiar with any of them, consult the stitch dictionary (page 24) and try the stitch out on a separate piece of fabric to make sure you understand how to do it.

To thread your needle, stretch the yarn between your fingers and fold it around the needle to form a loop. Slip the eye of the needle onto this loop of yarn. If the whole process gives you trouble, merely invest in a cheap needle threader which is available at sewing and notions counters.

Work with a hoop that is appropriate to the size of the fabric you're embroidering. Place the hoop so that there is enough material around the rim for the fabric to hang evenly. The cloth should be taut, like the top of a drum, across the hoop.

In smaller areas, of course, such as the collar of a shirt, it will be impossible to work on a frame; the embroidery will have to be done in your hand, without a hoop. In this case, make especially sure that the stitches are even, and when you are finished, iron your work, using a damp cloth.

Start at the center of the design, watching the work page and the color photograph carefully for color and stitch changes. Roll the portion of the fabric you are not working so that it will stay as clean as possible.

Secure each new thread by weaving it in and out of the yarn already worked on the back of the fabric. Do the same when you finish each thread. For the very first thread on the fabric, leave a long tail, and as soon as you have done a portion of work, weave that original thread into the back.

Use a thread that is about 18 to 20 inches long, and work in an even rhythm, with even tension. Always cut the yarn, never tear it. Follow the stitch instructions carefully. Don't feel rushed, but work with ease and pleasure. As in all embroidery, you are not competing with anyone, but should work at your own pace and to your own standards. Enjoy the crewel work, stitch by stitch.

The Stitches

For instructions on how to do each stitch, consult the stitch dictionary on page 24. Remember that embroidery stitches were originally developed for

quite practical reasons. Buttonholing was meant to keep the edges of the material from fraying. Herringbone was used to strengthen or to disguise the seam, darning to repair a worn surface . . .

There are probably several hundred stitches that have been adapted and used for crewel embroidery but most of them derive from or are variations of the fundamental stitches. There is no point in learning all these stitches, since it is much more important to have a good command of a few techniques than to know them all superficially and to be at a loss as to where to use them. Don't be ruled by the stitches and don't judge your work by the variety of stitches displayed. A piece in which only a few have been used can have an elegant simplicity, whereas too many types of stitches will usually break up the continuity of the embroidery.

You will soon learn that the same stitch will look quite different when you change its size, its direction, or the thickness of the yarn. Though stitch direction and color shading are quite important, they are usually suggested by the natural form of the shape that you are depicting. For example, in a leaf, the veins will give you the inspiration for the direction of the stitches. Though there are no rules about stitch direction, changes in direction will catch the light differently and will provide a variety of tone and texture. The direction will also help define the construction of the

work and to integrate the embroidery.

As you work, you will learn what directions please you and are logical and appropriate to a particular shape. Before starting to embroider any form, give yourself guidelines. With a very fine pencil, carefully indicate on your material the stitch direction. You will find that these guidelines are an invaluable help, almost as important as the stitches themselves.

As to shading, the important thing is to be consistent. Work from dark shades to light and vice versa, using your own eye and the color photograph to determine when to change shades.

Do not make your stitches too long or too short. Too long a stitch looks rather sloppy and will catch, just as stitches that are too short will break the design and give a feeling of restlessness to the entire pattern.

If you are a beginner or if you have not tried out a variety of stitches, I would suggest that you start your crewel work with a sampler of the stitches. I'm a great advocate of samplers both because they're a wonderful way to get total command of the stitches and also because they make a lovely decoration and are a good personal reference for the crewel worker.

Remember, in all these stitching instructions, it is not necessary to follow the work chart exactly for each design or color combination. Add as many of your own variations as you like.

Blocking

When your work is done, it must be blocked and finished. If you do a lot of embroidery, it is a good idea to invest in a blocking board. This could be a piece of wood or composition board which has enough give so that you can push tacks into it fairly easily. I use a piece of insulated wall board for this purpose.

Buy a piece of graph paper to the size of your board. Glue or nail it onto the board and then wrap the paper and the board with a sheet of plastic wrap. This will keep the paper from getting wet.

Make a mild solution of lukewarm water and Ivory soap. Working with a clean sponge, go over the entire fabric, on the right side, thoroughly dampening it. This will prepare your work for blocking and will also clean and freshen it. Do not press hard or rub your sponge too energetically over the embroidery.

Lay the embroidery face up on the board. Use the graph paper as a guide to keep the piece straight. Tack the embroidery down at quarter-inch intervals, through the taped border of the work, with rust-proof pins or upholstery tacks. Check as you go along to make sure that the edge of the area you are blocking coincides with the lines of the graph paper.

Checking

When the embroidery is dry, make sure that all the threads are securely fastened. Take a few strands of each color that has been used in the work and attach them loosely to the back of the embroidery. They will stay there for possible future repairs.

Mounting

You can mount your own work and, if you do, you should consult one of the very good books on the market specifically on this subject. If you like, you can have your work professionally mounted. More and more shops do this kind of work, and your local needlework shop or department store will either do it or refer you to someone who can.

After the work has been mounted or made up into a finished product, Scotch-guard it carefully so that it will stay clean. There is some controversy right now about the use of Scotch-guarding, since some people have been having difficulty with woolen yarns which have been so processed. I've used this kind of product for many years, though, and have had no problems.

Fashion Notes

Though decorative and functional embroidery has been with us practically since the invention of the needle, the fact is that embroidery seems to flourish in good economic times, when there is leisure time. In the past, people of wealth spent enormous sums of money on embroidered silks and velvets of all sorts. One example of this kind of display is to be found in the magnificent embroidered costumes of the court of Louis XIV.

In recent years, the designers of clothing and of home furnishings have continued to use embroidered fabrics. But there is a difference: we tend to have a much more casual view of where this sort of decoration belongs. Young people embroider their washed-out blue jeans; men's shirts are more likely to be embroidered when they're worn pool-side than at the Opera. Gone are the days when only ball gowns and velvet breeches bore fine handwork.

The same kind of more casual style holds in home furnishings. It would be very unusual to see in a contemporary home the kind of elaborate gold-thread embroidery that our grandmothers threw over their pianos. Instead, one might embroider a picture frame, an umbrella stand, or even a wastebasket.

We've done some sketches, which appear on pages 110 and 111, of the uses of embroidery in fashion and in home furnishings, all taken from the transfers. They are not meant to be patterns of what you should do or restrictions on the use of embroidery, but rather are intended simply to spark your imagination on the possibilities of using crewel embroidery in a creative way. Simply bear in mind that with the excellent man-made fibers now on the market we can make embroideries that will take both frequent washing and a great deal of wear and tear.

In well-equipped needlework stores and in department stores, one can find very interesting prefabricated clothes and furniture, manufactured specifically to be adorned with hand embroidery. Thus, you can buy a belt, all ready to embroider, and spare yourself the problem of mounting and finishing. There are lucite accessories, backgammon, chess and bridge table tops, Queen Anne chairs, footstools, handbags and many other items of this type available. All one needs to do is to finish the embroidery and insert it into the place that has been provided, or else cover one of these prefabricated items. The possibilities are unlimited, either using these commercial products or clothing and accessories of your own creation.

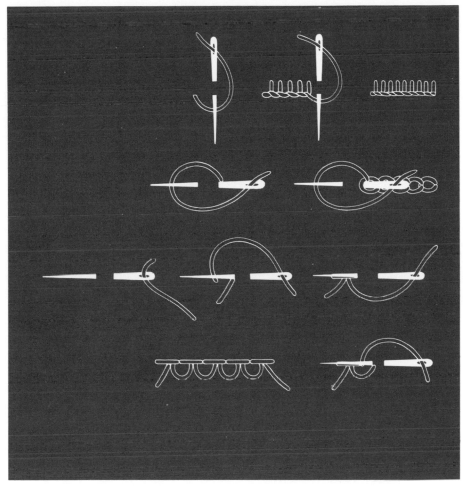

Stitch Dictionary

After you have consulted the work chart for the design you've chosen, look carefully at the diagram and text describing each stitch used. The stitch descriptions are arranged in alphabetical order.

The diagrams indicate with a * the beginning point of each stitch and will show you, step by step, how to do the stitch. The accompanying text gives you general information. It will, for example, indicate those cases where the stitch should be done from left to right or top to bottom. If there is no such indication, you can work in whatever way is most comfortable for you.

A complete listing of all stitches used and the page on which they are described is included below.

Bark Stitch

Lay down vertical rows of long stitches and tack them down with small stitches to form a pattern of parallel rows of the tacks. Used as a filling, it is most effective in varying colors and thicknesses of yarn.

step 1

step 2

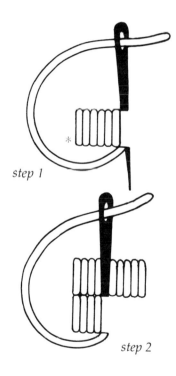

step 1

step 2

Block Shading

Block Shading consists of blocks of straight parallel stitches of the same length, in different shades of color. The length of the stitches in each block is the same, but it may vary from block to block. Make sure to draw guidelines, and work in horizontal rows from top to bottom of the form you're covering. Always bring the needle up on the same side of the shape to be embroidered, in the wrapping motion shown in Step 1.

Bokhara Stitch

This stitch involves tacking down long straight stitches with smaller ones whose position moves slightly from row to row to form a diagonal pattern. It takes lots of practice to make the diagonal rows come out even.

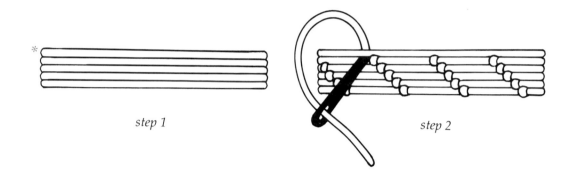

step 1   step 2

Bullion Knot

Begin with a backstitch as shown here, pulling the needle almost, but not completely, through the fabric. (Use a needle that has a small eye and a comparatively thick body.) Then wind the thread tightly around the tip of the needle (but not so tightly that it will be a struggle to pull the needle through), to cover the exact same length as the first stitch.

Finally, pull the needle through the coils and bring it back to the point where you started. In other words, the coils will now cover the empty space formed by your original backstitch. Make sure to hold the coils firmly while pulling the thread through. Although this stitch is tricky, it makes wonderful little sausage shapes.

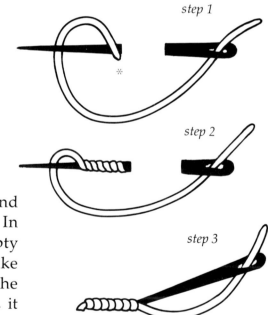

step 1

step 2

step 3

Burden Stitch

The Burden Stitch is used for covering and filling areas. Long parallel stitches are laid down horizontally about an eighth of an inch apart. Then they are overlaid with smaller, vertical stitches in contrasting color or fiber, spaced in alternate rows. Because it offers endless possibilities for shading and texture, I use this stitch whenever I can.

step 1

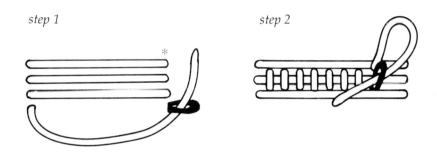

step 2

step 3

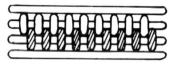

step 4

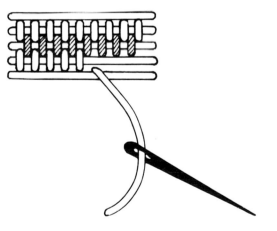

Buttonhole Stitch

Also called the Blanket Stitch, it is worked from left to right. Work evenly, with stitches of equal length. It is good for edging but can also be used as filling by working one row beneath the other, preferably in different tones of color. Step 3 in the diagram shows the stitch worked closely for a solid effect.

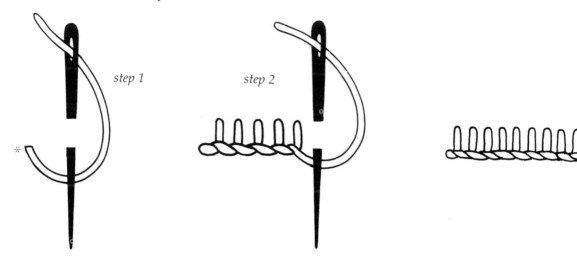

step 1

step 2

Chain Stitch

This is a versatile and frequently used stitch, which can be worked as an outline, a filling, or combined with other stitches. Work from top to bottom, and always complete each loop by inserting the needle exactly in the place it came up. It may take a little practice to keep the length of the loops even.

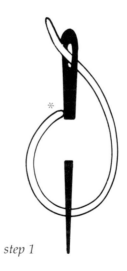

step 1

step 2

Cloud Filling

A pretty, lacy-looking stitch that is begun by placing tiny stitches in alternating rows at regular intervals on the fabric. Then, with a blunt needle, adjacent rows of these stitches are laced together with the same or contrasting color yarn. Do not go through the fabric when you lace. Different effects can be created by varying the spacing of the foundation stitches.

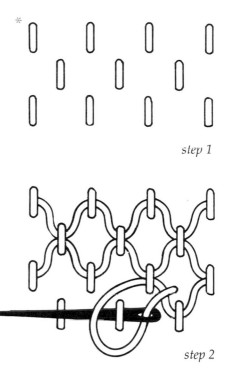

step 1

step 2

Coral Stitch

This stitch is a continuous row of knots, evenly spaced along a thread. Work from right to left, holding the thread taut, and pick up a bit of fabric with the needle each time you make a "coral."

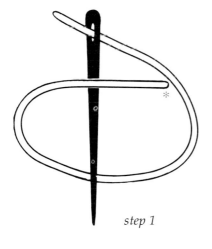

step 1

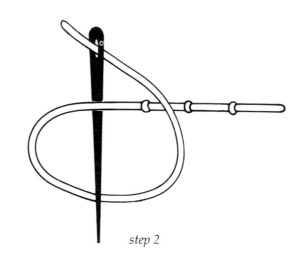

step 2

Couching Stitch

The basic Couching Stitch involves small straight stitches which tack down long threads in single or multiple strands. First, lay down the long thread, then work the tacking in the same color or another shade. When using rows of couching stitches as a filling, alternate the tacking stitches from row to row to form a regular pattern.

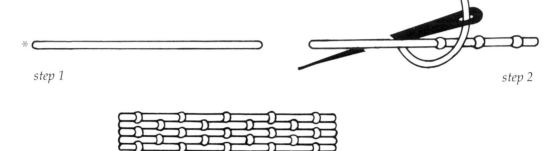

step 1   *step 2*

Cretan Stitch

This is a very versatile, textured filling stitch. As the diagram shows, work one stitch by looping the thread from the right, then make the next by looping it from the left. Stitches should be fairly close together, and the base of each should fall along a straight line.

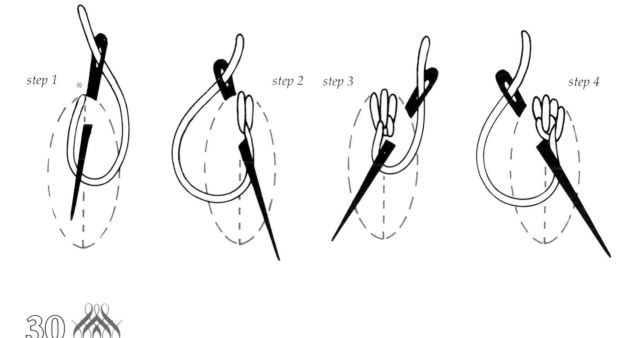

step 1   step 2   step 3   step 4

Cross Stitch Trellis and
Cross Stitch Knot Trellis

Lay a trellis of evenly spaced horizontal threads covered with vertical ones. At each point where these rows meet, place a good-sized cross stitch to tack down the intersection. Make sure all the overlapping stitches of the crosses go in the same direction. To make the Cross Stitch Knot Trellis, place a French Knot (page 33) in each square of the trellis. Use a contrasting color to form a really pretty design.

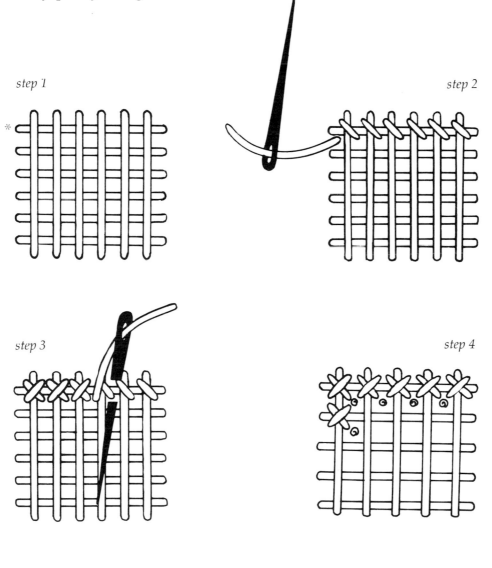

step 1

step 2

step 3

step 4

Ermine Stitch

The Ermine Stitch can be used as a light filling or as a border when worked in rows. First make a long straight stitch, then cover it with a long-legged cross stitch.

step 1

step 2   *step 3*

Fern Stitch

This lovely fernlike stitch can be used for leaf veins or sprays. Three straight stitches of the same length, one vertical and two slanted, radiate from the same central hole. The vertical stitches act as a connecting vine for the sprays of fern.

step 1

step 2   *step 3*   *step 4*   *step 5*

Fly Stitch

This is a light filling stitch that can be placed at random or in horizontal or vertical rows. The small bottom stitch holds the "v" in place.

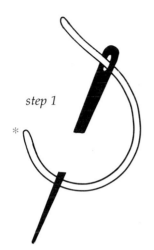

step 1

step 2

French Knot

My favorite advice to crewel workers is "When you don't know how to fill a space, use a French Knot." It can be used singly, in small groups, or even to cover a large space. Wind the thread once or twice around the needle—never more—fairly tautly, and bring the needle down through the fabric right next to where you came up. For a delicate effect, use a single strand; for a bold effect, double or triple it.

step 1

step 2

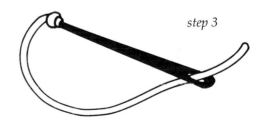

step 3

Fishbone Stitch

The three Fishbone Stitches—regular, looped and raised—are usually employed to work leaf shapes. They can also be used for borders or geometric shapes, in which case the stitches are worked in equal lengths and not graduated, as they are for leaves. If you are embroidering a design with many leaves, try alternating the different Fishbone Stitches for a varied effect and for texture.

REGULAR

Start the regular Fishbone with a straight stitch, then alternate, with the next stitch on the left, the following on the right, and so forth. Work all stitches from the same central line.

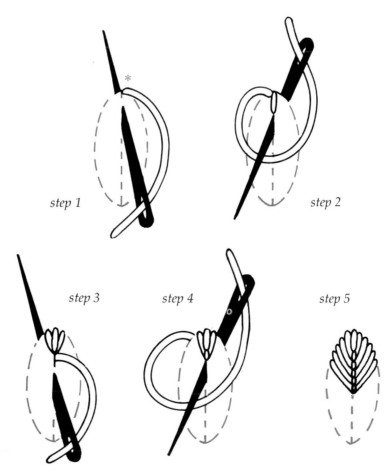

step 1   step 2

step 3   step 4   step 5

LOOPED

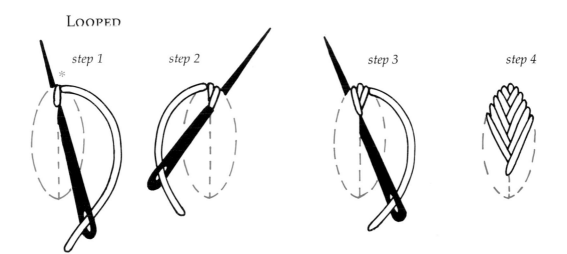

step 1 *step 2* *step 3* *step 4*

RAISED

In the Raised Fishbone, make especially sure to work the crosses very close together for a herringbone effect.

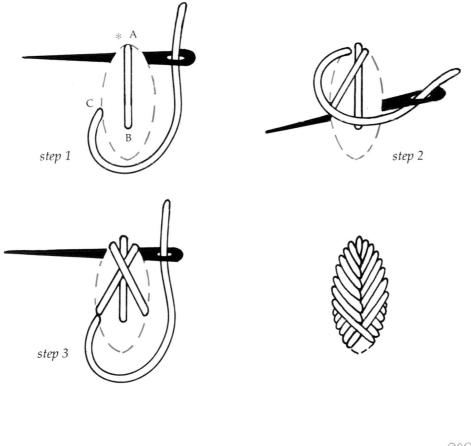

step 1 *step 2*

step 3

Laid Work

Laid Work consists of tacking down long stitches so that they won't snag. First lay the threads over the area to be filled, then go back and tack them down at practical intervals with any stitch that will hold the thread in place. The Chain Stitch, Split Stitch or Stem Stitch will do nicely. Where possible, use the tacking stitch decoratively, for example, to indicate veining on a leaf, or for color contrast.

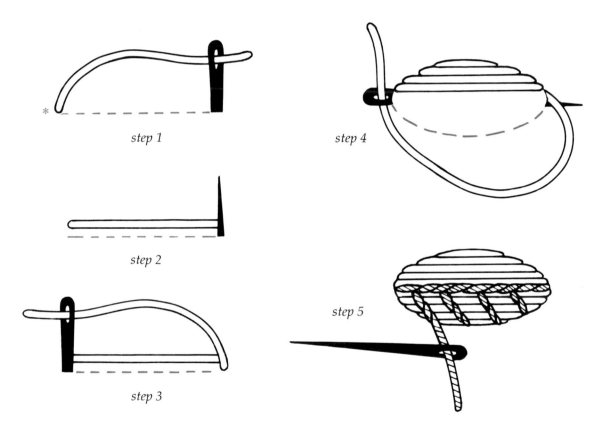

step 1

step 2

step 3

step 4

step 5

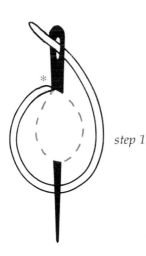

Lazy Daisy Stitch

This is a single loop stitch, secured at the bottom with a straight stitch. It can be worked singly, or arranged in groups like the petals of a flower.

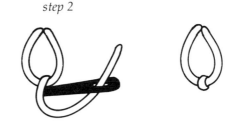

step 1   *step 2*

Long and Short Stitch

This crewel stitch requires practice but is worth learning because it allows you to "paint" on fabric. Working in horizontal rows, from top to bottom or from the outside of a form to the center, embroider the first line of stitches, using alternately one long stitch and one short.

Subsequent rows are worked in the long stitch only, but, the result is a staggered effect. Always do this work on a hoop using penciled guidelines and stitches that are neither too long or too short. In shading, always work from dark to light or light to dark to achieve a natural effect.

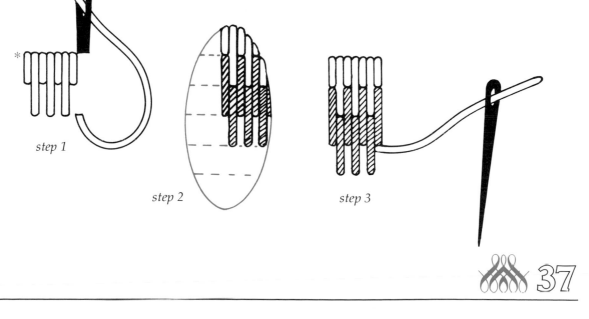

step 1   *step 2*   *step 3*

Pekinese Stitch

To work the Pekinese Stitch, embroider a very even row of backstitches. Then go back and loop through this row from left to right. The interlacing thread only goes through the fabric at the beginning and end of the work. Work uniformly. Do not pull the loops tightly, but hold them in place with your thumb.

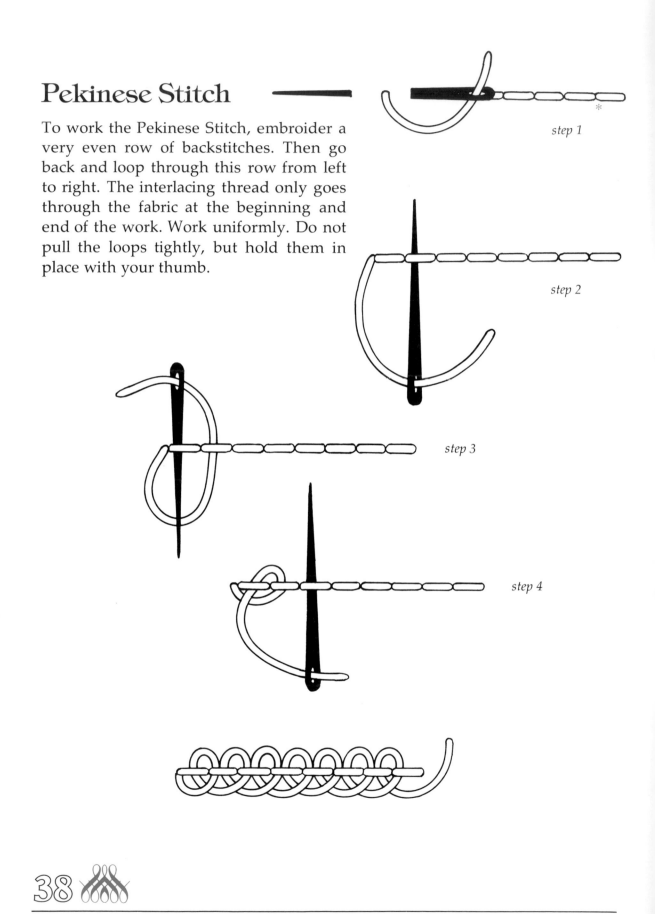

step 1

step 2

step 3

step 4

Reversed Satin Stitch

This very attractive stitch is worked by alternating rows of diagonally placed Satin Stitches (see page 41). It can fill vertical or horizontal shapes and, like the Satin Stitch, should be worked closely and evenly. It is very effective when done in yarns of varying thickness and tone, because the reversed blocks of stitches catch the light in such a way as to create different tones.

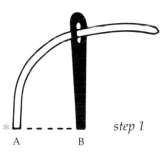

step 1

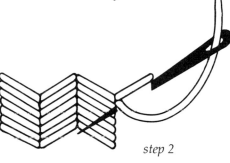

step 2

Roumanian Stitch

Make long horizontal stitches and tack them down with small slanted stitches which are of equal length. Move from left to right in horizontal rows, working from the top of the shape to the bottom.

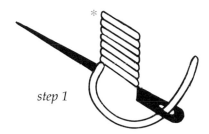

step 1

A   B

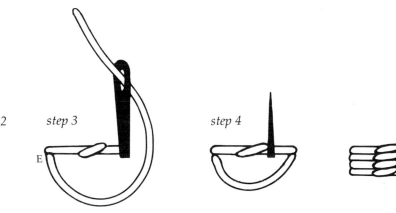

step 2

C

A   D   B

step 3

E

step 4

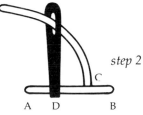

Rosette Stitch

Rosettes can be worked singly or continuously to make a border. Make sure they are all the same size by working with guidelines. Continuous rows of rosettes are difficult, since you don't tack them at the bottom. Make sure you hold them firmly in place with your thumb to avoid pulling the thread through and destroying the loop.

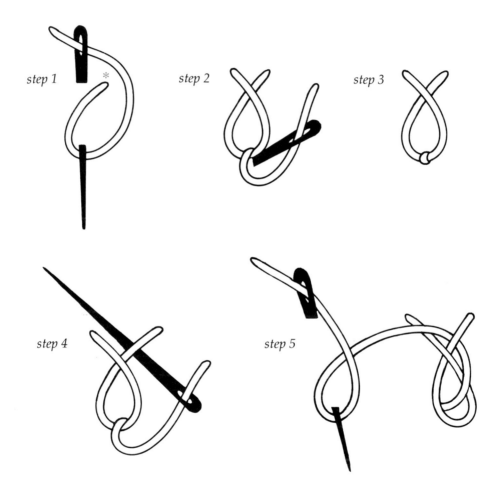

step 1

step 2

step 3

step 4

step 5

Satin Stitch and Padded Satin Stitch

The Satin Stitch lends itself to any shape and can be worked in one color or in shades. Work with penciled guidelines and practice before you begin your final embroidery. Make sure that the stitches are not too long or too short and that they lie close together. Remember that the needle is always brought up on the same side of the shape to be embroidered, in a wrapping motion. If you want a softer, three-dimensional effect, use the Padded Satin Stitch, which involves going back over the same area in the opposite direction.

If your pattern calls for a Straight Stitch, simply work one individual Satin Stitch along the guideline you are following.

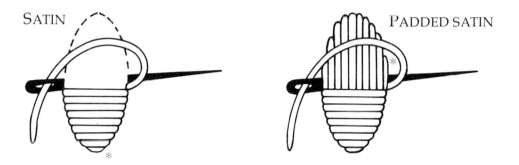

SATIN

PADDED SATIN

Sheaf Stitch

The sheaf filling stitch resembles little bows and can be regularly or irregularly placed in a given shape, depending upon the effect desired. First embroider three vertical stitches, then tie them horizontally with two small stitches placed close together, without going through the fabric.

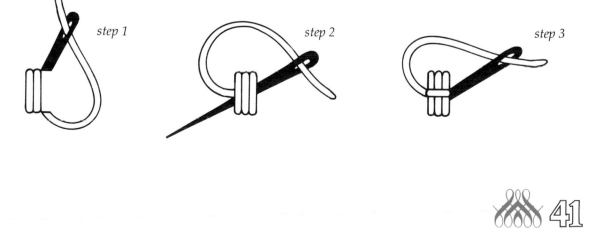

step 1

step 2

step 3

Spider Web Stitch

The Spider Web Stitches are very handsome circular designs. If a pattern calls for many webs, alternate the two variations shown. The first step is to establish a circular framework by stretching an uneven number (usually 7 or 9) of spokes in a circle. The spokes should be of even length. I stretch from 3 o'clock to 9, then 6 to 12, then 11 to 5, and 8 to 2. Finally, bring the needle up at about 2:30. Now move to Step 3 of the diagram and secure the spokes at the center. As in Step 4, weave the thread over and under the spokes (without going through the fabric) until the circle is completely covered.

To whip the spokes, work as in a backstitch, bringing the needle back one spoke, then forward two. Continue whipping until the circle is covered. It is very important to embroider the thread evenly and closely around the spokes for both variations.

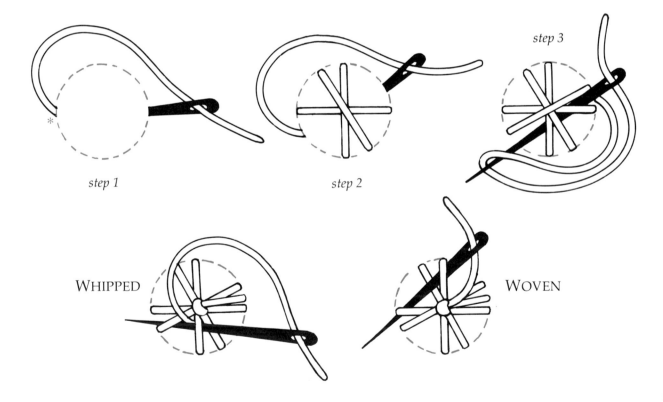

step 1   step 2   step 3

WHIPPED   WOVEN

Split Stitch

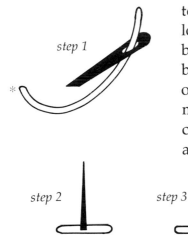

step 1

step 2

step 3

Those of you who have been warned all of your lives to be careful not to split the embroidery thread will love this stitch. Working with soft thread from top to bottom or left to right, make a straight stitch. Then bring the needle up through the fabric in the middle of this stitch and split the yarn. The Split Stitch makes a fine chain—the finest line you can make in crewel—and it can be used for outlining or for filling and shading.

Stem Stitch and Whipped Stem Stitch

The Stem Stitch is used for outlining or to fill a large area. Shading can be achieved by working the lines of stem stitches in several tones. Work from left to right, holding the thread consistently above or below the needle. Keep the stitches of even length. For a bolder line, work the Stem Stitch and then "whip" over it at evenly spaced intervals with yarn of the same or contrasting color. The whipping thread does not go through the fabric, but only loops around the Stem Stitches.

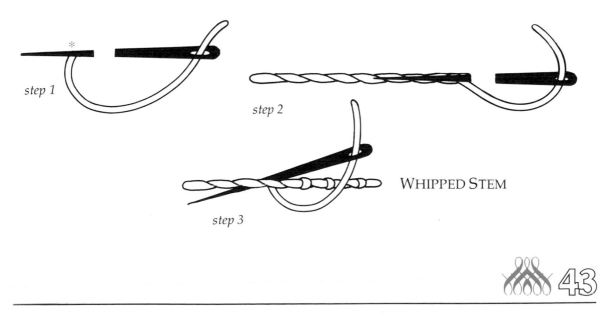

step 1

step 2

step 3

WHIPPED STEM

Straight Stitch

See Satin Stitch, page 41.

Turkey Work

This is a closely worked, looped backstitch. Start by picking up a piece of the material, as in Step 1, leaving a little tail of yarn. Throw the yarn above the line of stitches and bring the needle back one stitch and out in exactly the same place you began, as in Step 2. This secures the yarn. In Step 3, throw the yarn below the line of stitches, leaving a loop. In Step 4, secure it by throwing the yarn on top and bringing the needle back to the end of the loop. Work from left to right, forming loops and then securing them.

Note that you should have a continuous line of backstitches above a row of loops, as in Step 5. When you come to the end of a row, cut the yarn and begin a new row just above it on the left side of the work. After the space is covered, cut and trim the loops to the desired length. If you want to form small tufts, trim the loops down to a smooth uniform height. By using soft gradations of color, you can create a velvety effect.

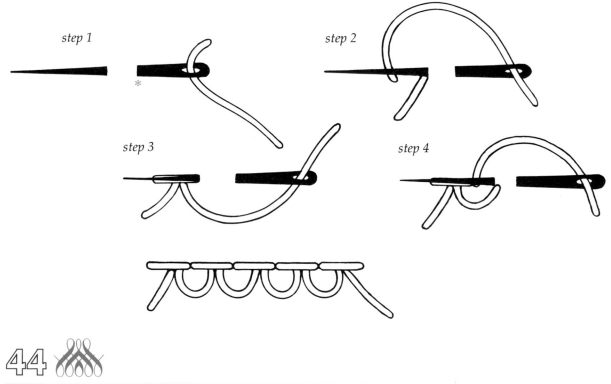

step 1

step 2

step 3

step 4

Weaving Stitch

Those of you who have repaired old socks will find the weaving stitch familiar because it really is nothing more than a darning stitch. Work a number of evenly spaced vertical stitches across the fabric and, with a blunt needle, alternately weave over and under these stitches, going through the fabric only at the beginning and end of each line. The best effect is obtained when different thicknesses and colors of yarn are used.

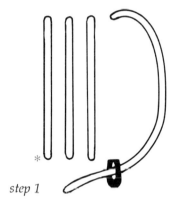

step 1

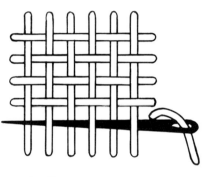

step 2

1 Buttonhole   3 greens

2 Split   3 yellows

3 Fly

4 French Knot

A simple floral pattern, good for a beginner. I have outlined the leaves with two rows and filled them with a scattered Fly Stitch for a delicate effect.

Color illustration, page 49

page 48

pages 50–51

page 52

 49

1 Chain 3 greens Rows of Satin Stitch form right side of this
2 Satin 3 rusts Jacobean leaf. Scatter Ermine Stitch in
3 Stem, Whipped background.
4 Sheaf

Color illustration, page 49

1 Satin
2 Split

1 orange
1 rust

If you want to simplify this rococo design, eliminate the background and trace only the letter onto your fabric, marking guidelines so that you achieve the correct slant. All the letters require the same two simple stitches. Though we have shown only an "L" in this pattern, *every letter* of the alphabet appears on a transfer at the back of the book, as well as on pages 108 and 109.

Color illustration, page 49

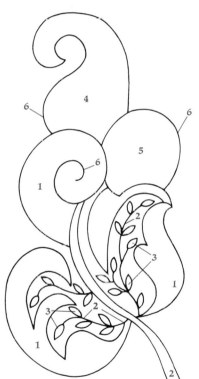

Color illustration, page 49

1 Satin
2 Chain
3 Lazy Daisy
4 Cross Stitch Knot
   Trellis
5 Reversed Satin
5 Stem, Whipped

5 blues

This design is nicest when done monochromatically, in varying shades of one color. Texture is achieved by using several stitches. The latticework at the top is a closely worked Cross Stitch Knot Trellis. Make sure to keep all the stitches short in this fine work.

1 Satin	2 blues
2 Stem	4 greens
3 French Knot	2 pinks
4 Ermine	1 yellow
5 Fishbone	

A summery design. Alternate Satin Stitch direction for each side of the petals for realistic effect. Scatter the Ermine Stitch inside the leaves. Three to six rows of Stem Stitch outline the leaves. All green leaves on pink flowers are done in Fishbone.

Color illustration, page 49

page 54

page 55

pages 56–57

1 Long and Short	2 blue-greens
2 Fishbone	3 pinks
3 Split	3 reds

A romantic, nostalgic pattern that could be adapted for many uses. All the roses are done in Long and Short. Work one petal at a time, varying the shades as indicated in the color photograph.

Color illustration, page 53

© Comptoir de l'Industrie Textile de France

1 Stem, Whipped	3 greens	Lacy flowers and leaves create a rich de-
2 Chain	1 orange	sign by the use of light stitchery, rather
3 Buttonhole	3 pinks	than solid fillings. Most of this pattern is
4 Satin	1 turquoise	done in the Whipped Stem Stitch, with all
5 Stem	1 white	the stems in Chain.

Color illustration, page 53

1 Long and Short	2 blues
2 Chain	3 greens
3 Buttonhole	1 magenta
4 Satin	1 orange
5 Fishbone	3 peaches
6 Bokhara	2 pinks
7 French Knot	1 white
8 Cross Stitch Trellis	2 yellows

The Boussac fabrics are extraordinarily beautiful. Many are of Jacobean origin. I have adapted a few of them to crewel embroidery. You might remember, when you want to create your own designs, that textiles are a rich source of inspiration.

This pattern has a good deal of open space, which makes a lovely, airy design. Use good clear colors. All the white flowers are done in Chain Stitch, as are the stems and those leaves indicated on the chart. The small leaves at the bottom are done in Fishbone Stitch.

Color illustration, page 53

1 Split   2 blues

2 Fishbone   3 greens

3 Satin   2 reds

4 French Knot   2 yellows

5 Coral

6 Buttonhole

7 Long and Short

8 Cross Stitch
   Trellis

A naïve but traditional American pattern that would be charming as a chair seat or picture where a period accent is desired. All the veined leaves are done in Fishbone. The yellow flowers are worked from the outside toward the center in close rows of Split Stitch.

Color illustration, page 60

1 Satin	1 blue
2 French Knot	1 green
3 Stem	1 orange
	1 pink
	1 yellow

This is a simple repeated pattern. You can use as many or as few units as you like. Make sure the stitches in the flower petals lie close together.

Color illustration, page 60

page 59

page 58

page 61

1 Satin	3 blues
2 Split	2 magentas
3 French Knot	1 white
	2 yellows

Another good beginner's piece, this pattern employs only 3 stitches. We have outlined the blue flowers with 3 rows of Split Stitch, and the centers are solidly filled with French Knots. In working the Satin Stitch petals, as always, vary the direction of the stitches.

Color illustration, page 60

1 Stem
2 Buttonhole
3 Fishbone
4 Split
5 Satin
6 Spider Web
7 French Knot
8 Bullion
9 Turkey Work
10 Chain

1 blue
3 browns
1 gray
3 greens
2 reds
1 white
2 yellows

This is an adaptation of the famous medieval unicorn tapestries. You can, if you like, personalize the embroidery by stitching your initials and the year in the space left around the tree trunk.

Make sure to draw guidelines for the leafy Satin Stitch on the bushes. You may be searching for the Spider Web Stitches in this design — they are in the centers of the palm fronds. The bunny tails are done in Turkey Work, which the rabbits don't seem to mind. When you are embroidering the animals, try to have the stitch direction simulate their sinews and shapes.

The collar around the unicorn's neck is worked in Stem Stitch on top of the stitches which form the animal. I used one strand of yellow and one of blue, twisted together.

Watch for the Bullion Knots, which appear only in one blue flower at the bottom right.

Take your time with this pattern — it will surely become an heirloom.

Color illustration, page 64

page 65

pages 62 – 63

page 66

| 1 Fern | 1 green | An old-fashioned, delicate pattern that could be |
| 2 French Knot | 2 pinks | worked in silk for an even finer effect. It could |

1 Fern   1 green

2 French Knot   2 pinks

An old-fashioned, delicate pattern that could be worked in silk for an even finer effect. It could be used as a picture frame or a mirror, or you could use this spray as a border on clothing or linens. Always remember that if the fabric is going to be laundered you should use a man-made fiber or a strong cotton.

Color illustration, page 64

		This pattern and the buttercup look lovely
1 Buttonhole	1 brown	together and would make a nice pair of pic-
2 Split	3 greens	tures. The flowers are done in Buttonhole
3 Fishbone	2 yellows	with a close-worked French Knot. All leaves
4 French Knot		are done in Fishbone.

Color illustration, page 64

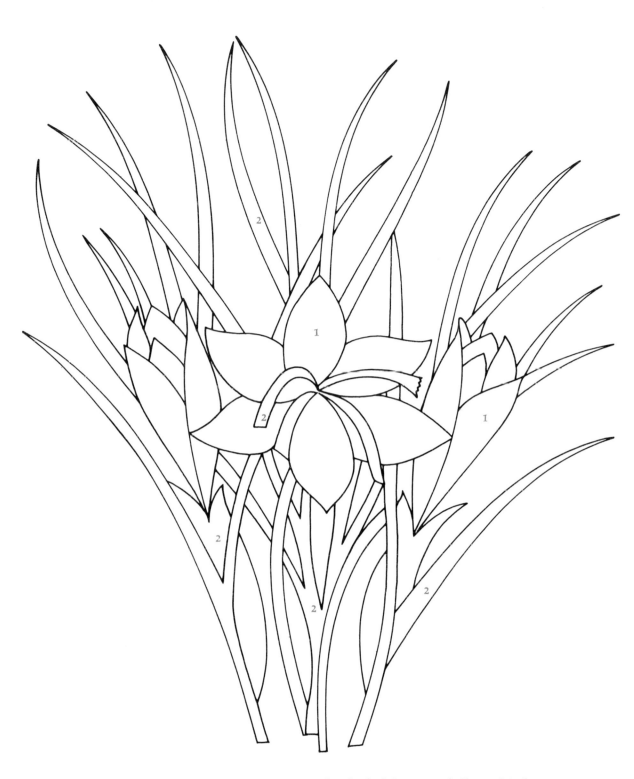

1 Long and Short   4 blues   Freely shaded Long and Short Stitches are
2 Stem   4 greens   worked along guidelines for this rather ar-
                     1 orange   chitectural flower.
                     1 yellow

Color illustration, page 69

1 Split	1 black	I have used this pattern for cushions on a
2 Stem	1 green	pair of antique chairs, and the effect is
3 Chain	1 light purple	romantically elegant. All the flowers
4 Fishbone	2 pinks	should be worked in Split Stitch from the
5 French Knot	1 yellow	outside toward the center. All leaves are
6 Satin		done in Satin and the stems are in Stem
		Stitch.

Color illustration, page 69

page 67

page 68

page 70

1 Long and Short
2 Stem

4 greens
4 pinks
4 purples
4 reds
4 yellows

The tulips embroidered on this tea cozy will truly give you a chance to paint with your needle and thread. All the flowers are done in Long and Short, with a free use of color and shading.

Color illustration, page 69

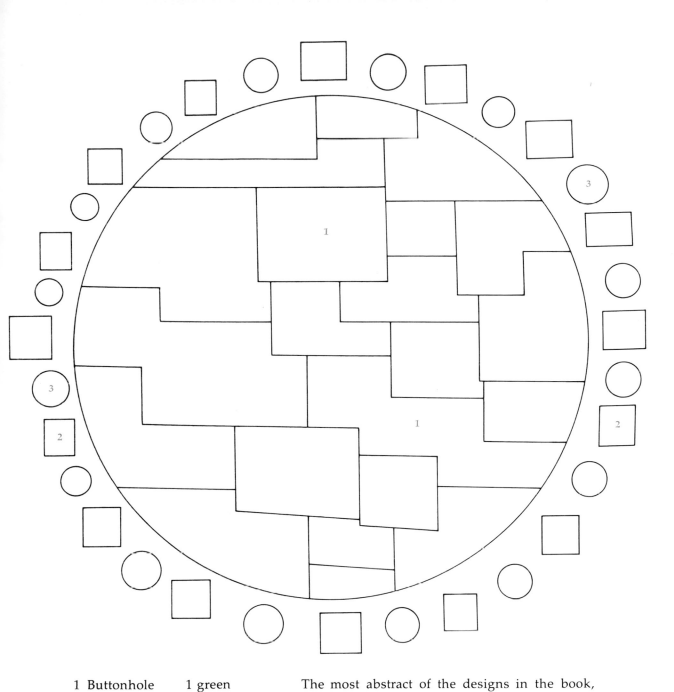

1 Buttonhole	1 green
2 Satin	4 oranges
3 French Knot	1 yellow-green

The most abstract of the designs in the book, this pattern is an indication of how you can use geometric clusters of stitches to form innovative designs. Although the horizontal part of the stitch is covered by the subsequent row, the geometric shapes in the circle are done in a close Buttonhole Stitch. This gives a wonderful undulating texture. Of course you could do it in blocks of Satin Stitch, but you would lose the movement.

Color illustration, page 73

1 Split   2 browns

2 Satin   1 green

             1 white

             2 yellows

A pattern to use in a casual setting, it employs only 2 stitches. You could work the corn in purples, for a striking Indian corn effect.

Color illustration, page 73

72  **CORN**

EASY

page 71

page 72

page 74

1 Satin	1 blue
2 Straight	5 greens
3 French Knot	1 yellow
4 Stem, Whipped	

This is one of the few designs in which I have used a double strand to achieve a bold, textured flower. You could, if you like, use a single strand for more delicacy.

Color illustration, page 73

1 Stem
2 Chain
3 French Knot
4 Satin
5 Buttonhole

6 Weaving
7 Long and Short
8 Fishbone
9 Fly
10 Rosette

4 blues	2 pinks	
2 browns	2 reds	
4 greens	3 yellows	
1 magenta		

You might want to embroider your initials at the base of this tree. The trunk and limbs are stitched very lightly to accentuate the flowers and bird. The raspberries are filled solidly with French Knots.

Color illustration, page 77

1 Satin	1 black	
2 Buttonhole	1 gold	
3 Split	1 green	
4 Cross Stitch	1 pink	
Trellis	1 red	
5 French Knot	1 turquoise	
6 Straight	1 yellow	

Here crewel stitchery is used to achieve a folk-art effect. We've done it on a classic, plain blouse where it provides a colorful contrast. The Straight Stitch indicated in the leaves is, of course, a single Satin Stitch.

Color illustration, page 77

1 Long and Short	1 black	A charming, grandmotherly design. The
2 Fishbone	1 blue	Roumanian has been worked in different
3 Chain	4 browns	directions for a woven basket effect. All
4 Roumanian	2 golds	the flowers are done in Long and Short in
5 French Knot	3 greens	closely matched shades of each color.
6 Split	3 pinks	
7 Satin	2 purples	*Color illustration, page 77*
	3 reds	

1 Satin   1 green   This is a modern adaptation of a very
2 Fishbone   1 magenta   old crewel design that a beginner can
3 French Knot   1 purple   easily do and quickly finish.
4 Stem

Color illustration, page 77

1 Satin	1 brown
2 Fishbone	3 greens
3 Straight	2 reds
4 Stem	1 white
5 French Knot	

A clean, elegant pattern that is appropriate to modern or period settings. Note that only the leaves with a center line are done in Fishbone; the rest are done in Satin Stitch. When working the Satin in a round form like these berries, start at the center, work one side and then the other. Flowers are always worked from the outside, toward the center.

Color illustration, page 81

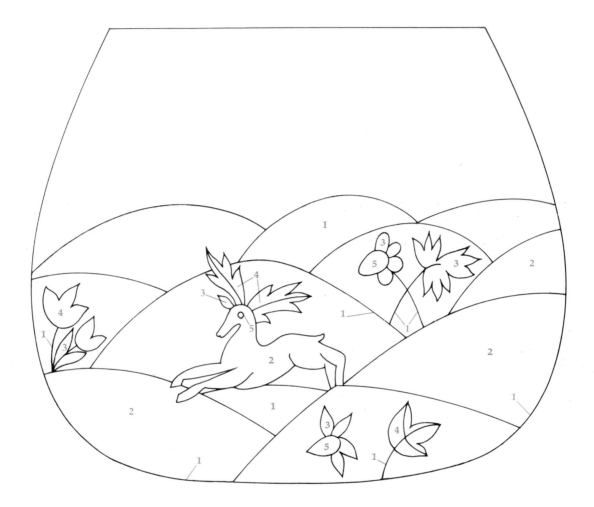

1 Stem
2 Long and Short
3 Satin
4 Fishbone
5 French Knot

1 beige
3 browns
1 ecru
1 gold
4 greens

Lots of movement is achieved in this pattern, through the use of these typically Jacobean hills which offer both dimension and motion. Some of the hills are done in Long and Short, some in Stem Stitch, and some are only outlined with stitches. Shade the deer lovingly, as Mother Nature did.

Color illustration, page 81

1 French Knot	2 browns
2 Long and Short	2 golds
3 Split	4 greens
4 Stem	1 olive
5 Fly	1 yellow-green

In this structured, charming design it is easy to achieve a very disciplined-looking embroidery. Clusters of French Knots form the blossoms. The leaves are open at the base and scattered with Fly Stitches.

Color illustration, page 81

1 Fishbone
2 Stem
3 Satin

1 black
1 brown
3 greens
1 ecru

Work the leaves in a double thread and the pear in a single to achieve a lovely bas-relief. The pear is done in Stem Stitch, starting at the outside and working toward the center. Make sure to keep your fabric taut on a hoop or the pear will pucker.

Color illustration, page 81

page 86

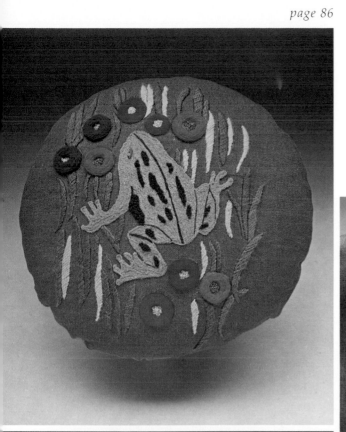

page 87

page 88

1 Satin
2 Split
3 Spider Web
4 French Knot

1 blue
2 browns
2 greens
1 magenta
1 red

This is a cheerful and amusing piece for a child. All the leaves are done in a slanted Satin Stitch. Don't attempt them without guidelines. The flowers are formed by a very loosely worked woven Spider Web Stitch. You might even want to try it in a double strand.

Color illustration, page 85

1 Stem
2 Bark
3 Pekinese
4 Coral
5 French Knot
6 Split

2 beiges
2 greens
2 pinks
3 rusts
1 yellow

A wonderful design for children. We have made this simple pattern more interesting by using a variety of stitches. Notice how closely the Pekinese Stitch is worked in the mushroom. It almost has a knitted texture.

Color illustration, page 85

1 Fishbone	1 black
2 Stem	3 greens
3 Satin	1 magenta
	1 red

Use two strands for the leaves and one strand for the apple, to get contrast in texture. The apple is done in a Stem Stitch, from the outside toward the center. Work with fabric taut on a hoop, preferably on a closely woven fabric. This pattern, of course, works very well paired with the pear shown on page 81.

Color illustration, page 85

page 90

page 91

pages 92 – 93

1 Long and Short
2 French Knot
3 Fishbone
4 Satin
5 Laid Work
6 Bokhara
7 Stem

1 black
3 blue-greens
1 brown
3 greens
4 reds

This somewhat time-consuming project results in a rich piece of embroidery. Each berry has been separated from the others by outlining in the Stem Stitch. The French Knots are superimposed after the berries are done in the Long and Short stitch. The leaves are alternately embroidered in Laid Work and Bokhara.

Color illustration, page 89

1 Satin
2 Stem, Whipped
3 French Knot
4 Cross Stitch
   Trellis

3 blues
1 magenta
3 pinks

I used this design as a centerpiece on a large tablecloth, but you might use it on the corners of the cloth, on a pillow or even on the back of a shirt. Start the blue circles at the center, working first one side then the other. The centers of the flowers are done in closely worked French Knots.

Color illustration, page 89

1 Long and Short	2 beiges
2 Chain	2 browns
3 Block Shading	1 gray
4 Buttonhole	1 rust
5 French Knot	1 white
6 Stem, Whipped	
7 Split	

Though this is a rich, ornate design, leaving certain areas unfilled has lightened the total effect. Though crewel is generally thought of as brightly colorful, it is very elegant in an elaborate pattern like this one to keep the color tones fairly subtle.

The white flowers surrounding the design are outlined in 2 rows of Split Stitch. Note how Long and Short stitches have been used on some of the flowers in a single color.

Color illustration, page 89

© Comptoir de l'Industrie Textile de France

1 Split	2 beiges
2 Buttonhole	4 browns
3 French Knot	1 dark blue
4 Satin	4 greens
5 Roumanian	1 light blue
6 Couching	1 red
7 Fishbone	5 rusts
8 Rosette	1 white
	1 yellow

The hills allow freedom for your needle to leap in both color and stitchery. The entire deer is done in close rows of Split Stitch, following the animal's structure and shaded. Feel free to simplify or combine stitches for the hills.

Color illustration, page 96

1 Satin
2 Fishbone
3 Burden
4 Buttonhole
5 French Knot
6 Bullion
7 Stem
8 Split

1 beige
3 browns
1 gray
8 greens

A fanciful fairy tale you can embroider. The leaves with a line in their center are done in Fishbone, the others in Satin Stitch. The French Knots on the top hills are outlined in a Stem Stitch. Bullion Knots are irregularly placed in the open hills.

Color illustration, page 96

1 Fishbone
2 Stem
3 Long and Short
4 Buttonhole
5 Turkey Work
6 Burden
7 Satin
8 French Knot

2 blues
3 greens
2 magentas
1 purple
5 rusts
4 yellows

A funny little partridge in an elegant pear tree makes a very cheerful design. Watch carefully the shading of the tree trunk. Note that the pears are well defined by outlining in Stem Stitch. The partridge's breast is done in a close Turkey Work, the wing in Burden Stitch in several tones.

Color illustration, page 96

This sampler of repeated animals is not necessarily meant to be done on one piece. You could take a single animal and embroider it on a pocket or purse, or use a row of animals as a border. Make a children's fantasy by taking one of each group or use it as it is in your country kitchen.

ANIMAL BORDER, DEER AND SKUNK INTERMEDIATE

1 Split
2 Bokhara
3 Satin
4 Stem, Whipped
5 French Knot

1 beige
1 blue
2 browns
4 greens
1 magenta
2 oranges

This border could be split in two, using the animals alone, or the leaf arabesque by itself. The animals are shaded in a Split Stitch. Outline the leaves with a Whipped Stem Stitch.

Color illustration, page 96

1 Long and Short
2 Split
3 Bokhara
4 Straight
5 Satin
6 French Knot

1 beige
2 browns
3 greens
2 rusts

The tails of these wonderful creatures have gotten their fluffiness by using layers of Straight Stitches radiating from the center of the tail. The colors of the yarn have been mixed at random.

Color illustration, page 96

1 Long and Short	1 black	Here you can see the attractive effect of
2 Reversed Satin	2 browns	a Reversed Satin Stitch on the wings
3 Satin	1 gray	and tail of the birds. Instead of doing
4 Split	3 greens	the leaves in Fishbone, we have used a
5 Cretan	1 pink	closely worked Cretan Stitch.
6 French Knot	2 reds	
	1 white	*Color illustration, page 96*
	2 yellows	

  **WILDFLOWERS**

ADVANCED

1 Long and Short   1 black
2 Stem   2 browns
3 Satin   1 gray
4 French Knot   3 greens
5 Turkey Work   1 olive
6 Cloud Filling   1 orange
7 Laid Work   3 purples
8 Fishbone   1 red
9 Buttonhole   3 yellows
10 Straight

The artistry of shading these flowers is a great goal to aim for. The Long and Short Stitch is used here as a tool of painting and shows the individuality that can be achieved in crewel.

The veins in the Laid Work leaves are here done in a Stem Stitch. The yellow buds on the right are worked in Cloud Filling.

In shading any of the flowers or stems, feel uninhibited. Work the colors freely. In crewel, as in nature, all greens go well together, as they should on these leaves.

Instead of filling the gray flowers in, shadows have been achieved by the use of French Knots, artfully placed.

Color illustration, page 104

page 105

pages 102 – 103

pages 106 – 107

1 Buttonhole   4 browns
2 French Knot   4 rusts
3 Stem   1 white
                4 yellow

I love the drapes we've made with this rustic pattern, worked in fall colors. Contrary to what we usually do, these leaves have been embroidered from the center out.

Color illustration, page 104

POPPY

ADVANCED

1 Stem
2 Long and Short
3 Satin
4 French Knot

1 black
1 blue
4 greens
1 magenta
4 pinks
1 purple
4 reds
2 turquoises
4 yellows

This is another pattern where you shade freely, and don't worry about where colors "belong." All the flowers have been done in Long and Short; all the leaves in close rows of Stem Stitch. To make the heavy stems more interesting, we varied the shades of green.

Color illustration, page 104

See pages 49 and 51 for the color photograph and specific design instructions for working these letters. They can be used on pockets, at the bottom of embroideries and wherever else you want a monogram.

108 ALPHABET

EASY

FASHION IDEAS

For Clothing

For the Home

THE TRANSFERS

Sheet 1 contains transfers for the following patterns: Boussac, Beau Soleil (page 55); Carnations (page 68); Floral Fantasy (page 74); Rabbit and Tree (page 95); Partridge in a Pear Tree (page 97); Wildflowers (page 102).

Sheet 2 contains transfers for the following patterns: Alphabet (page 51); Folk Border (page 59); Crocus (page 67); Tree of Life (page 75); Berry Branch (page 80); Pear (page 84); Frog (page 86); Corn (page 72).

Sheet 3 contains transfers for the following patterns: Leaf (page 50); Swirl (page 51); Liverwort (page 52); Fern (page 65); Flower Basket (page 78); Floral Antique (page 79); Deer on the Hills (page 82); Strawberries (page 90); Boussac, Cybele (page 93); Leaping Deer (page 94).

Sheet 4 contains transfers for the following patterns: Buttercup (page 48); Boussac (page 57); Pennsylvania Birds (page 58); Jasmine (page 66); Tulips (page 70); Calico Flowers (page 76); Artichoke Blossom (page 83); Snail (page 87); Poppy (page 106).

Sheet 5 contains transfers for the following patterns: Rosebuds (page 54); Free Flowers (page 61); Unicorn (page 62); Geometrics (page 71); Apple (page 88); Elizabethan Flowers (page 91); Animal Border, Deer and Skunk (page 98); Animal Border, Squirrels (page 100); Animal Border, Birds (page 101).

About the Author

Lisbeth Ransjö Perrone is one of the world's most talented needlewomen. She is the author of the beautiful and best-selling NEW WORLD OF NEEDLEPOINT and A NEEDLEPOINT WORKBOOK. Born and educated in Sweden, Ms. Perrone also studied in Paris and graduated with a degree in the decorative arts from a Swedish school. She teaches at the American Embroiderers' Guild of which she is a director and her work has appeared in museums and exhibits throughout the country. She lives with her son in New York and in Sweden.